Random Memories

By Rikki Ford

DORRANCE
PUBLISHING CO
EST. 1920
PITTSBURGH, PENNSYLVANIA 15238

Dorrance Publishing Co
585 Alpha Drive
Pittsburgh, PA 15238
Visit our website at www.dorrancebookstore.com

ISBN: 979-8-88683-506-9
eISBN: 979-8-88683-594-6

Biographical Sketch

Ricki Ford

"Rikki Ford" (a pen name and nickname) was born in Ferndale, Michigan on January 22nd, 1941 as Margueritha Ford. It was not until 1958 that she became a model and show girl (dancer), first working in the "Idlewild Revue" produced by Arthur Braggs.

In 1961, she joined "Larry Steele's Smart Affairs Review." The show worked Atlantic City and traveled extensively throughout the country. This lasted for the next seven years.

Ms. Ford is not unfamiliar with a well-kept appearance along with grace and poise—the elements that make even the plainest person beautiful. She attended and graduated from one of Michigan's most recognized schools of cosmetology, has studied dance, modeling, and is an instructor who has taught cosmetology, manicuring, advanced hair styling, and hair weaving. Ms. Ford has received meritorious awards in the field of permanent hair relaxing, hair coloring, and even silhouette styling. She also received her cosmetology teacher's certification.

Ms. Ford has been a Jet Magazine Centerfold model over half dozen times, has modeled designer clothing, modeled at the Detroit Automobile Shows, and was selected as one of the finalists in the Miss Michigan Universe Pageant. Rikki is also a recipient of a certificate of basic seamanship from the 19th District Coast Guard Auxiliary.

Rikki has written articles for a National Beauty Magazine, is the author of a Cosmetology Word Sleuth book on Cosmetology, and an author of a 2005 children's book "Robber Rat." She was once the co-owner and Educational Director of a beauty school and a barber school.

Rikki has studied sign language and is recognized by the State of Michigan as having had the first beauty school in Michigan to offer Cosmetology and Manicuring to the Hearing and Speech impaired. She has also written articles on sign language in Cosmetology.

Random Memories

Mitcheldale, that is the name of the street I lived and grew up on. Maybe it should have been called a road because it was not paved back then, just mud and rut holes. Sometimes after a heavy rain, it would be so muddy with the rut holes becoming deeper that the young men that visited from Detroit would park their cars on Eight Mile Road, wear boots and walk to our house. The city boys coming to court the country girls of Eight Mile Road.

There was a saying back then by the guys from Detroit, "Man, you better be careful of those girls from Eight Mile Road. They can work 'VO Do' with their thang, man. You have sex with one of them, then you are hooked and walking them muddy roads and getting your ass kicked by one of those gangs, the Dukes or the Shakers."

Our house sat on a few acres of land with a large garden of string beans, corn, tomatoes, greens, blackberries, plum trees, and grapevines. There were chickens, pigs, two goats, a horse, a Shetland pony, and always dogs. I heard my father made and supplied the neighborhood with some of the best corn liquor and wine.

My mother was music. There was always music in the house. We had a piano, and my mother played every day. My grandmother (Mom's mother) taught piano and played for her church.

I heard my father enjoyed taking Mom places where there was a piano. He would have her play. She could read and play all kinds of music, and was always buying the latest sheet music. My father would have ,om play boogie-woogie music. The people would dance and rave about how well Mom played. This would make my father proud. He enjoyed showing her off while making himself the life of the party.

I grew up and went to school with "The Spinners." They were also from the Eight Mile Road area of Ferndale, Michigan, Royal Oak Township. We were friends and they spent a lot of summer nights on our front porch, singing. Guys like Billy Henderson, Crathman Spencer, Pervis Jackson, Henry Franbrough, and two brothers, Herbert and Walter Gains, and the Dixon brothers. This was before they became "The Spinners."

I think Billy and I had a crush on each other back then. I also remember having a class in Grant School (Mr. Ford's class) with Henry Franbrough and Pervis Jackson. Pervis sat near me and used to write me love poems. One poem started out, "How much do I love you? I love you like a tree…" I can't remember the rest. Just think, I hear Pervis has written love songs for the group. Somehow the guys in the group back then became separated and then there were two sets of singers. One group remained "The Spinners" with Bobby Smith joining them as lead singer. The other guys called the new group the "Originals." The Gaines, two Dixon brothers, and Crathman Spencer. I went into show business before the Spinners became famous and worked on shows with some of the top entertainers of the time, but I never became a popular show business name. "The Party would last for seven years."

Mom sent me to a charm class through the YWCA. I took classes on how to sit and walk like a lady. She was very much the feminist and wanted us girls to possess those same qualities of

"Always a Lady." Mom was also talented with her sewing machine and made us girls beautiful clothes.

She would take us to a clothing store, and we would show her the expensive clothes we liked but couldn't afford most of the time, because there were three of us girls. She would buy the color material we liked, go home, and make the same dress.

Mom's sewing, the charm classes, and her insistence on young ladies developing pleasing personalities made us Ford girls a little popular among the Detroit Jet Set and the pacesetters of that time.

The fashions of the day were stovetop hats with the crease down the center and two dips in the front, the Stetson hats, and the Stetson shoes. The ladies wore Carman Jones skirts. All the fellows had to have shirts with the Billy Eckstine collar and hand-painted ties and usually bought them from King Brooks.

The hairstyles from that era were back in the 1980s and 1990s, later called pencil waves. In the 1950s, the hair artists were Benny Mullen, Whitmore, and Shaw. The waves were called a "process" or a "do." Working men wore their "do-rags" to help protect those waves so they would last during the week and still be looking good for the weekend.

Being raised just outside of Detroit, I also grew up with the Michigan Chronicle Newspaper. I've been on the front page of the newspaper and featured in pictures throughout the Chronicle over the years as an entertainer. I've enjoyed and danced in the bright lights all over the world. A real joy has been to see so many local Detroiters and Eight Mile Roaders become successful as educators, professionals, and entertainers.

Another singing group I remember and grew up listening to was Smokey Robinson, Ronnie White, Pete Moore, and Bobby Rogers who made up a group known as the "Matadors" who later became known as the "Miracles." Claudette Rogers-Robinson,

Gwen Whitmore, Jeanette Rogers, and Margie Etchinson-Braxton (who is now one of Detroit's top judges) became the "Matadorettes." I remember buying the Michigan Chronicle every Wednesday evening to find out what I had missed in the different social circles. Mainly I wanted to know what entertainers were in or coming to town, where they would be appearing, and with whom.

There were dances in the Twenty Grand Ballroom with big bands; the sound of Maurice King, Jimmy Wilkins, Choker Campbell, and, of course, Levi Mann. Local dancers were "Lottie the Body" and "Black Velvet."

Clubs like the Latin Quarters, Phelps Lounge, Flame Show Bar, Club El Sino, Elmwood Casino in Canada, the Gotham Hotel, and Sonny Wilson's club were the in-places or the "Hot Spots." At the Paradise Theater (with dancing on the mezzanine) you could see a live show complete with chorus girls and top-name entertainers, such as Sammy Davis, Billie Holliday, Cab Calloway, Charlie Parker, Slappy White, Redd Foxx, and Lionel Hampton.

There was the West End Jazz Clubs to hear Dizzy and Miles and, of course, our local talents – Kenny Burrell, Berry Harris, Teddy Harris, and Richard "Pistol" Allen (two of my favorites), Clark Terry, Donald Byrd, Yusef Lateef, Wendell Harris, Roy Brooks, and so many, many more.

The Graystone Ballroom was known for great ballroom dancing that only Detroiters can do with their own amicable styles. You can see some of these same ballroom dancers at clubs like "Reggie's" and Chuck's Millionaires Club on special nights of the week. There were dances called the Madison, the fully, Gully, the chicken, the Mashed Potato, and the Dog.

I hear the guys at the dance clubs really enjoy it when they find a lady who can really follow the steps. The ballroom dancing is so smooth with the lady following the leader's every move. Graceful movements of two bodies moving together as one. Definitely an art, like sheer poetry in motion. After the clubs closed, visits to the after-hours jazz clubs were in order. One was on Dexter, called the "Minor Key," and it was really unique.

In a club on Grand River called the crystal, every Sunday a line could be seen a block long. The club was small. They gave two shows to accommodate everyone. There were entertainers such as "Three Sounds," "Illinois Jacquet," and Gene Ammons.

Today I believe my brother-in-law, Henderson, has the best collection of jazz artists I have ever seen or heard.

After hours, you could also see the biggest cars in town parked at Top Hat and the White Castle Hamburger Havens (seven for a dollar).

Radio personality Frantic Ernie Durham was the rapper of radio. He could make everything rhyme. He could make the weather report come out in rhyme. Ernie D was on Soul Station WJLB, where WQBH now resides.

I remember listening to Jazz with Disc-jockey Leroy White, Ed Love, and Martha Jean the Queen. I heard she moved on to become the station program director. One of Detroit's favorite blues men, was J Butler also on WQBH.

In the fall, all the young men were on their way to the Brewster Center to watch the basketball games. Everyone tried to outdress each other, and each guy tried to have the prettiest girl on his arm. Buying a car from the handsome Seven Million Dollar Man Phil Townsend.

Arthur Braggs came to Detroit. He was a big numbers man from Saginaw, Michigan. He also ran a nightclub in Idlewild, Michigan. Idlewild was some of the Detroiter's summer resort and Braggs produced a live show each summer at the Paradise Club. There was a saying about Idlewild that "Idlewild was the place for idle men to meet some wild women."

Arthur Braggs' Paradise Club and Phil Giles' Flamingo Club attracted such name talent as Sarah Vaughn, Dinah Washington, and Bill Doggett. Many Detroit entertainers got their start there, including Della Reese, Jackie, Wilson, and the Four Tops. Three of the Four Tops married three chorus girls they met in Idlewild one summer.

Romance seemed to fill the air in the days of Idlewild, which was always crowded. So crowded until on those party weekends some people would sleep in their cars. The partying never stopped. After the two nightclubs closed down at 2:00 a.m., entertainers and guests would end up at the El Morocco Club after-hours where they would dance and sing until daybreak.

Everyone was welcome in Idlewild. Visitors came from all over Detroit, Chicago, Indianapolis, Cleveland, and even as far away as New York and California. I heard that the town's streets were named after these cities. When I talk to some of the old timers, they speak of visitors such as Joe Lewis, Richard Hatcher, and even Detroit Mayor Coleman Young.

Comedian Jackie "Moms" Mabley was a favorite performer in Idlewild. So were singers Jackie Wilson, Jerry Butler, Aretha Franklin, Sarah Vaughn, Della Reese, B.B. King, and the Four Tops, whose talents helped boost Detroit's Motown record label to pop music royalty.

Some of my favorite entertainers I met while working in Idlewild. One was Jerry Butler. He was so shy back in the 1950s in Idlewild. We used to play cards after the show many nights.

Arthur Prysock (Big Brother Prysock) always looked out for you. He loved to cook. Oh boy, how he could cook. I remember eating wonderful, well-seasoned, soul food meals he had prepared. When the show went on the road, the members of the show would chip in money and Arthur would grocery shop and cook. How all of us enjoyed those good soul food meals.

Comedian George Kirby fascinated me with the amount of food he could eat in one meal's sitting. When we finished a show his restaurant order would sound something like this. "I'll have one chicken." The waitress would ask, "You mean one chicken dinner?" George would say, "No, I mean one whole chicken." Then, George would add, "Greens, cornbread, lemonade, potato salad, and one sweet potato pie." The waitress would ask, "A piece of potato pie?" George would answer, "No, I want one whole sweet potato pie."

If you had the pleasure of George's company that evening, you had better be prepared for the gas that followed. Sometimes he would be silly, go into the next room, and make the gas sound, like a trumpet playing,

Bill Doggett came to work in Idlewild one summer in the 1950s. He and his band were there for four or five weeks. Bill Doggett's drummer was Eagle Eye Shields.

"It's showtime!" someone would call. Lights, music, and the show begins featuring Bill Doggett's band with Eagle Eye on the drums. Out comes the show girls, out comes the dancers.

One of the show girls does her featured spot and, as she makes her way back upstage, her eyes meet the eyes of the Eagle. Drumbeats start to sound to her every move. The show girl is Rikki Ford, a tall redhead from Eight Mile Road just outside of Detroit. Night after night as Rikki does her routine, the drumbeats catch her every move.

The drummer and the show girl dancer are creating a sexual excitement that the audience and chorus feel. Eagle Eye and Rikki on stage (stage lovers). Many loves started in Idlewild. Levi

Stubbs, lead singer of the Four Tops, and Clineice Townsend become man and wife. Arthur Braggs and show girl dancer Carlean Gill fall in love.

Braggs was in Detroit looking to hire dancers and show-girls for the summer season. Three months working at the resort club. This had to be the perfect three-month vacation, a job of fun, parties, and in the limelight as part of the stars of the show.

I was recommended to Braggs by Ziggy Johnson. Ziggy was working as an emcee at the Twenty Grand Club in Detroit. Ziggy also owned Ziggy Johnson's School of Dance and taught dancing.

Ziggy was a pioneer of show business in Detroit. He was a man of artistic courage and inspiration to so many of Detroit's young talented Blacks. He was also a favorite in the night entertainment circle, being the producer and emcee of nightclub acts, among them the "Flame Show Bar," the "Hobby Bar," and the Idlewild "Paradise Club" in the summer months.

My father had died and my mother was raising the five of us alone. At a young age and just out of school, I convinced my mother to let me join the show, but she only agreed after she made Braggs become my legal guardian, signing papers that he was responsible for my well-being.

Another producer of the Idlewild days was Phil Giles, Sr. Phil Giles owned the Flamingo Hotel and Night Club in Idlewild, Michigan. George Philip Giles was his name. He was born in Ocala, Florida in 1903. I hear he came to Detroit in 1923 and went into the hotel business in 1947. Later, he went into the hotel and nightclub business in Idlewild, Michigan in 1949. It is said that he helped pioneer Idlewild into one of the finest resort areas in the country. He was a member of various organizations; Lot Owners Association, Detroit Idlewilders, Idlewild Chamber of Commerce, and the Rotary Club of Baldwin, Michigan. I heard he was even the Mayor of Idlewild from 1951 to 1959. Phil Giles died in Detroit in 1963.

It had been about three years with the Idlewild Revue. The show has traveled after the summer season, to places such as New York, working at Wilt Chamberlain's nightclub. I dated Wilt while dancing at his club. There was a picture in Jet magazine as publicity. The dates were nothing serious. Wilt was very popular with a lot of ladies.

We worked at Basin Street in Boston. The show was there when the news came on TV about the death of President Kennedy.

We worked in Cleveland, Ohio at a club where I met Jim Brown. Jim was, of course, the star football player with the Cleveland Browns at that time. Mr. Brown had come to see the show. He sent someone backstage to invite me to have a drink with him after the show. I did go over to meet him, but I did not stay for the drink. I had accepted a date with another ballplayer, a basketball player at the time, and he was waiting to take me for breakfast. It was later that I found out that Jim Brown was offended by me not expecting to get acquainted. My date and I went to a restaurant. Surprisingly enough, this must have been the hot spot to go after the clubs closed because as my date and I were being seated, so was Mr. Brown and his date.

I felt uncomfortable some of the time as I looked across to where Jim Brown sat. It seemed to me that he didn't like the idea of me refusing his attentions. Now a big movie star, he probably doesn't even remember this. The evening did turn out to be enjoyable. As we sat waiting to be served, my date, who was a very handsome, tall gentleman who played basketball with the Harlem Magicians, took out a jewelry box and gave me a present of a necklace and earrings. He put the necklace around my neck and the rest of the night was beautiful.

The show was booked in Chicago a number of times at the Roberts Show Lounge. Those were always good times with the club being packed and sold out every show.

What a summer that first summer was for me in Idlewild: the rehearsals, the bright lights, pretty costumes, and attention from all the men. I think I could have become one of those wild women if it weren't for Braggs and Ziggy.

Ziggy choreographed the show and was also the emcee. Daddy Braggs, as I called him, and Ziggy by now were so damn overprotective of me. I would try and sneak out after the shows. They would always make me go back to the cottage rented for me, which I shared with two other girls in the show.

I remember one night I tried to sneak out, but as I turned and started to leave, there was Daddy Braggs and Ziggy. They had climbed up on a box outside the window and said to me (which scared the hell out of me), "Now just where do you think you're going?"

I did get to date some, but only with the guys Braggs approved of. I think before he let me date them, he must have threatened them, because on almost all the dates these guys were perfect gentlemen and never got out of line very much. When the show went on the road the rest of the year, Braggs taught me a lot about the fast life, the nightlife, about the night people of pimps, and how to take care of myself.

We worked in a club in Kansas City called the Black Orchid club. The club was on the corner of 12th Street and Vine. I dated the well-known Bar-B-Q King of Kansas City. They called him the strutting man. I guess they called him that because of that fine strut of a walk he had. Handsome Ollie Gates, the Bar-B-Q King, owner of Gates Bar-B-Q.

I had another date with Ollie as recently as the 1980s. We met up again in Las Vegas. The strutting man was older, but still fine and had what it takes to show a lady a great time. As recently as 2004, I saw Ollie on the Martha Stewart Show. Still looking good.

Time for a break.

The show returned to Detroit. "The Idlewild Revue." Time to prepare for the summer season, new choreography, new costumes, first-class costumes with personal fittings in New York. Costumes by top designers. Of course, we partied in New York those days and nights of costume fittings. It was wonderful going to the top New York nightclubs to see the big stars on stage.

We later worked in a nightclub in New York owned then by Wilt Chamberlain, the basketball star. I did date Wilt back then a couple of times. Now I hear he states he has dated quite a number of women in his time. Well, I guess I really don't remember anything special or anything spectacular to write about on either date (and I did stay the night).

Back to Detroit to start rehearsals. We rehearsed mostly at Ziggy Johnson's School of Dance.

One year Daddy Braggs visited Mexico. He hired eight dancers that traveled and danced with us for six months. This was a very interesting and exciting time. We were learning Spanish and the Mexicans were learning to speak English with city slang.

NIGHT LIFE IN CHICAGO

Arthur Braggs' "Idlewild Revue of 1962" very proudly introduces the world-famous Leon Escobar Dancers of Acapulco, Mexico, currently appearing at Roberts Show Club in the super production.

THE POSSESSED (African Ritual)

In the land of the Ruanda Urundi, located in the very heart of the mysterious Belgian Congo, are the tribes of the Watusis, African warriors, who are believed to have descended from the old Egyptians. These people celebrate their ceremonies with rites that surpass all of the other tribes of the Black Continent.

Let's turn our imagination so we are transported and introduced to the mystery and beauty of the Jungle. Let's hear the tom-tom of the African drums which announce a great pagan ceremony that we will be able to see by penetrating through the darkness of the night.

Beautiful African maids held prisoners deep in the jungle are freed by their captors and dance under the magic powers of the night. After their dance, they go back to their cages and disappear in the darkness.

Two young lovers of the Kikuyu tribe dance under the sacred tree to purify their love, and go to offer their future children to the god of the birds and leopards who governs their loves from the top of Mt. Mikeno.

The dance of the lovers is interrupted by the minister of the tribe who sings and presents the rites of an African wedding.

The newly married couple dance before the witch of the tribe who plays a very important role in this ceremony. He calls the gods of the earth and heaven, and makes all the members of the tribes become possessed by his black magic, so that the souls of the newlyweds may be liberated from the evil spirits in accordance with the mysterious African rites.

After very much research and study, Leon Escobar and his company have been able to present a modernized version of the ceremonies without taking away from it all the beauty and mystery of the real ceremonies and dances of Africa.

Idlewild Revue worked at a theater in Chicago called the Regal

Theater. A tall, handsome man came backstage. His name was Larry Steele. He was also a Black entertainment producer of a large variety show, "Larry Steele's Smart Affairs." A much larger show than the Idlewild Review. They were basically the same type of show with dancers, show girls usually a comedian, and a featured star. The producers of both shows were Black and the only two large shows of their kind.

Top Black entertainers usually got their chances for stardom from appearing and working with these shows. One of our show girls left the Idlewild Revue and joined the Steele show and what do you know; the next show girl to leave was me.

Just as the base summer show was Idlewild for "The Idlewild Revue" the base for "Larry Steele's Smart Affair" was the summer months in Atlantic City, New Jersey, Club Harlem. This meant moving on up the road, working with bigger stars, fabulous costumes, and more money.

Atlantic City, the boardwalk, the fabulous stores. I remember dating a wonderful guy from Baltimore, Maryland. Each time he visited Atlantic City, he would always take me shopping. I don't know any woman who doesn't want her man to take her shopping. When we went on these shopping trips, the sky was the limit. He would just hand me his wallet and I would buy anything I wanted. It seemed all the men I dated over the years were always very generous. I guess I have had almost all the material things a woman could want a man to buy her: clothes, diamonds, cars, furs, homes, but money can't buy true love.

I really enjoyed working at club Harlem in Atlantic City. with Larry and Braggs being the only two Black producers of these types of variety shows, I got a chance to work with a lot of the same stars from time to time and became friends with many. Pearl Bailey had also started taking her show on the road.

Working with Larry Steele Show

Larry Steele. He was "The Man Who Created the Action," "A Show Business Pioneer," and "A Man of Strength and Intellect." The renowned producer of "Smart Affairs Revue" a production lavished with stars, lots of laughs, beautiful girls, and rhythm, rhythm, rhythm.

I think The Larry Steele Show was designed principally to glorify the beauty and the talent of the Black Woman.

Every night on stage, Larry would say, "The American Black Woman was like a beautiful flower garden. They came in every color, size, and shape." In every show, there were songs like "A Pretty Girl" or "The Lady Has Class" Larry would sing.

Larry was a very high-principled man, but his imagination out-raced his finances many times. In those days, backers for the show were hard to find. There were days when club owners closed doors in his face. They would say things like, "Personally, I would like to book your show, but I'm afraid my customers wouldn't like an all-Black show." But nevertheless, Larry made headline triumphs from coast to coast, country to country.

Larry made it the hard way, but like most people say, "The hard way is the true way." (The trials and tribulations, the factory of success.) For example: In the 1950s, Larry took "Smart Affairs" to Miami Beach. It was for an engagement at the Cotton Club that was an all-Black show. At first, off stage, everything was really bad. The groups were forced to commute back and forth from a Black hotel in Miami to Miami Beach by bus and enter the Cotton Club by the back door. Larry was pretty mad about this, but he never permitted himself to show it. He was too cool and imaginative for that.

Instead, he contacted a famous columnist, Walter Winchell, and told him about "Smart Affairs." He invited him to see the show. Winchell really talked about the bigotry. People crowded into the Cotton Club. Many were Black and were surprised when they arrived and discovered the racial barriers had been lowered. Today the Miami Beach area is the most liberal of the south, and you must pay tribute to Larry Steele for being responsible for some progress.

Finally, in the late sixties, "Smart Affairs" came to an end. Larry Steele died. But "Smart Affairs" still lives on in the hearts of many.

Many of the great name entertainers either started out in Larry's "Smart Affairs" or at one time or another appeared with the show, those appearances contributing I am sure to both their fame and fortune. Among them are Sammy Davis Jr., Sam Cooke, Billy Daniels, The Orioles, Freda Payne, Peg Leg Bates, Sonny Payne, Do Mita Jo, Al Hibbler, Lavern Baker, The Platters, Adam Wade, The Treniers, Lou Rawls, George Kirby, Dick Gregory, Moms Mabley, Aretha Franklin, and Leslie Uggams. In fact, Lola Falana got her singing start with Larry Steele. She was in the chorus line and Larry heard her sing and started letting her sing on the breakfast shows.

The breakfast show was a show that started at six a.m. for all the night people in Atlantic City.

Well, just pick a name. The odds are they appeared with "Larry Steele's Smart Affairs" somewhere in the world.

My friend "Sir Lionel"
He had a wonderful act. He was often featured on "Smart Affairs." He painted his fantastic, well-built body (Gold) all over from head to toes. He would dance with special lighting. "Truly Fascinating."

Larry Steele Smart Affairs Revue hotel, night clubs, and concert appearances:

El San Juan Hotel, San Juan, Puerto Rico

Latin Casino, Cherry Hill, New Jersey
Dunes Hotel, Las Vegas, Nevada
Deauville Hotel, Miami Beach, Florida
Club Harlem, Atlantic City, New Jersey (every summer, all summer long)
Beverly Hilton Hotel, Beverly Hills, California
Flamingo Hotel, Las Vegas, Nevada
Elmwood Casino, Windsor, Ontario, Canada
Waldorf Astoria Hotel, New York, New York
Masonic Auditorium, Detroit, Michigan
Bill Miller's Riviera, on Broadway New York City

(Larry Steele Smart Affairs Revue hotel, night clubs, and concert appearances – continued)
Thunderbird Hotel, Las Vegas, Nevada
Three Rivers Inn, Syracuse, New York
Conrad Hilton Hotel, Chicago, Illinois
Syria Mosque, Pittsburgh, Pennsylvania
Sugar Hill, on Broadway New York City
Barclay Hotel, Toronto, Ontario, Canada
Casaloma Night Club, Montreal, Quebec, Canada
Keil Auditorium, St. Louis, Missouri
Copa City, Miami Beach, Florida
Memorial Hall, Dayton, Ohio
Faisan Bleu, Montreal, Quebec, Canada
Hotel Sherman, Chicago, Illinois
Academy of Music, Philadelphia, Pennsylvania
Civic Opera House, Chicago, Illinois
Carnegie Hall, New York, New York

Television and Theatre appearances:
Milton Berle Texaco Star Theatre, NBC

ABC Special Telecast, ABC
The "Tonight Show," NBC
Summertime on The Pier, CBC

(Larry Steele Smart Affairs Revue Television and Theatre appearances – continued)
Tivoli Theatre, Chicago, Illinois
Apollo Theatre, New York, New York
Milgram Circuit, Philadelphia, Pennsylvania
Regal Theatre, Chicago, Illinois
Shea Circuit, Ohio and Pennsylvania
Howard Theatre, Washington, D.C.
Uptown Theatre, Philadelphia, Pennsylvania
RKO Theatre, Midwest States
Leading Theatre of Australia, New Zealand, and the Far
East

It's amazing how much love one heart can hold. I have so much love for so many people I have met and worked with during my years in show business.

Skip Trenier is definitely one of the many. I shared so many good times with Skip, one of my first loves. I remember one night after a show at the Club Harlem, in Atlantic City, New Jersey. It was The Larry Steele Show, of course, featuring the Treniers. Nancy Wilson was also working in Atlantic City at the time, and after her show, she had come by Club Harlem just as our show ended for the night. She had come to see Skip and possibly share some time, but Skip didn't accept the invite and left the club with me. I think she and Skip had some dealings in the past because as Skip and I left the club, Nancy followed us outside and cursed us both out (in good old street fashion). I never did get the real understanding of that night. Skip refused to talk about it. We just continued talking and she continued cursing.

Also during that year, there was usually a three-some. Skip Trenier, Kelly Isley of the Isley Brothers, and me. I really enjoyed being with the both of them. They both treated me so special. Very sad, sad day when I heard Kelly Isley had passed.

I remember another great lady singer, cursing me. Believe me, I really never did anything that was intentional. Dinah Washington was appearing at the Flame Show Bar in Detroit. I was having a great time waiting for the show to start because I was really looking forward to hearing Dinah sing. Just before the show started, a few guys came over to my table, and a few more, and then a few more. The show started but the men didn't sit, they just kept talking to me. The guys were being rude and should have seated themselves. Dinah refused to start her show because of the noise. She said, "Rikki Ford, you big yellow bitch. I'm the star of this club, and it's time for me to do my motherfucking show." The whole club became silent. The men at the table seated themselves and all eyes were on me. I really didn't know what to do or say, but all eyes were on me, so I took advantage of the situation. I was seated in front of the stage, so I just stood right up, turned to the audience, took a bow, and sat down. The club laughed and became quiet. Dinah never said another word. She just stood there and looked. I looked back and smiled. She sang great as usual. I've always liked and enjoyed Nancy Wilson singing and I also felt the same about the late Lady Dinah Washington.

Al Hibler used to amaze me, on how he could tell when a certain person would walk by him. I used to think he just couldn't be blind. Maybe he could smell you. (Smile.) I worked on the same show with him quite a few times. Each time I would walk past him, he would always call my name.

Della Reese and I had a thing for the same guy once.

Drummer Larry Rice. Fine, fine Larry Rice, seems like I must have had a thing for drummers. I eventually married a drummer in Detroit. Maybe something to it, the way the drummer knows how to keep the "right beat," on stage and off.

A good friend and favorite drummer is Richard (Pistol) Allen. Remember I said, my friend. That means I didn't give the drummer some. We went to see "Redd Foxx Show" while our show was on break. Got embarrassed again, as usual. Waiting for the show to start, a few of the fellows came over to my table. Some, sure enough, fine like Detroiter Buddy Rose (The Black Prince), Reggie Alexander, or Bennye Mullen. Out comes Redd Foxx. The guys are still standing at the table. Redd Foxx said, "Now ladies and gentlemen, that's how you can tell when a woman's got a good thang. Look at all them motherfuckers over there standing around that table. Rikki Ford, I know that thang's good. Need to give Redd some. Sit y'all hungry asses down. Don't none of you know what to do with that kind of thang." The show went on with Redd Foxx talking about what you supposed to do. I was so insulted but what can you expect when you go to one of Redd Foxx's shows?

Sammy Davis, Jr. would come to Atlantic City to work with the show at Club Harlem for two weeks during the summer season. Mr. Davis would work those two weeks and donate some of his salary to the NAACP.

Sammy was so kind and very generous to all of us. He was married to Mia Britt at the time. I remember her coming to visit Sammy. One day before she left, Sammy sent for me and another show girl to come to his dressing room where he introduced us to his wife. I never really understood why because that is all it was, an introduction.

The next week, after Sammy's wife left, I was sitting backstage in the dressing rooms that the show girls shared. They were upstairs behind the stage. There was also a payphone backstage. This night, Sammy had invited everyone in the show to join him for breakfast, his treat. Well, I didn't go. I really didn't feel much like being one of the crowd following Sammy Davis.

The next thing I remember is a chauffeur coming backstage and saying Mr. Davis had sent his car for me. He said, "I'll be waiting for you out in front of the club." I told him, "No, thank you. I don't really feel like being one of the crowd. Anyway, I do like to be asked and given the opportunity of saying yes or no." I think the chauffeur was quite surprised. He asked again, "You really are not going to go?" I replied, "I said no, thank you, didn't I?"

This time he left, giving me that smirk of a smile again. Just as soon as I dressed and was leaving, the backstage phone rang. I started not to answer it since I was the only one left backstage. However, back up the stairs I went and answered the phone.

The voice said, "This is Sammy Davis, is Miss Ford backstage?" "Yes, this is Miss Ford," I answered. "Miss Ford, will you join me for breakfast?" I told him I was not hungry and that I had just sent his chauffeur back. He was very insistent and asked again. He said, "If you are not hungry, then just come for coffee." I finally accepted and he asked if he could send his chauffeur back for me.

As we entered the restaurant, I noticed the only empty chair was next to Mr. Davis in the center of the table. All eyes and heads had turned and followed me as I was seated in that empty chair. There was silence and then gradually the table chatter resumed.

There was a bike ride on the boardwalk. On occasion, I stayed overnight in one of the suite of rooms at the hotel as a lot of people did. There was always cab fare in the drawer of several hundred dollars. Mr. Davis was always very generous.

Before Mr. Davis left that summer, I was given my first mink stole.

Sammy also made a dream come true for one of the dancers that summer. The dancer's name was Lola Falana. Larry Steele took me with him one night to a local club in Atlantic City. We went to the club to see a dancer Larry had heard about. The dancer was Lola Falana. Larry liked her and he hired her. She joined the show right away as one of the dancers in the chorus line.

The dancers were called ponies and sometimes there were ten to fifteen female and two to four male dancers. The chorus line would dance, then the show girls came on with slower dance routines and fabulous gowns and hats.

Every Sunday morning at 6:00, there was a breakfast show. This gave all the entertainers in town from the other clubs in Atlantic City a chance to see the show. Most times, one of the stars that was appearing in the city would come up on the stage and sing, prompted by the audience.

Lola could always be heard singing in the dressing rooms. It was at one of these breakfast shows that Larry let her sing. This was the first time he had heard her sing as a professional on that breakfast show. Sammy knew how well she danced and now he was very impressed with her singing. The next thing we all knew, Lola was on her way to stardom. She joined Mr. Davis in the show "Golden Girl."

Arthur Braggs' "Idlewild Revue" and "Larry Steele's Smart Affairs" would both work in Las Vegas.

I remember working at the Thunderbird Hotel in Vegas. There were about 25 of us in the cast. We were not allowed to congregate in the casino between shows, nor were we allowed to eat in the restaurant between shows. We were told that it would become too crowded with our cast members, and it would inconvenience the tourist trade. So, we were given a large room up some stairs, away from everything it seemed like, where we had special waiters and waitresses that took our orders and waited on us each night.

By the time the cast finished eating, it was always time for the show. I often wonder if this was done just so there was no large gathering of Blacks in one place in the hotel because we were also told not to gamble between shows.

Since those days, I have visited Vegas a number of times. Sometimes with "Larry Steele's Smart Affairs" and sometimes on my own.

One visit was in April 1992. I was invited to attend a commemorative birthday party which was a "Tribute to Duke Ellington's 93rd." This affair was sponsored by the "ladies who danced" and was held in the Trianon Ballroom of the Stardust Hotel in Las Vegas.

Some of the guests present were Debbie Allen and her husband Paula Kelly, Baby Sanchez Davis (Sammy Davis' mother), actor Greg Morris and his wife, Easter Roole, clineice Stubbs, wife of Levi Stubbs of the Four Tops, Carlean Gill, Betty Williams, Betty Boo from Detroit, Jeri Steinberg from Denver, Prince Spencer, and so many, many more.

The entertainment for the night was the talents of Frances Nelly from California, Reverend 0.c. Smith, Bunny Briggs (dancer), Ernie Andrews, singing Jazz Norma Miller, and Cholly Atkins.

Great old times returned to Detroit when the Ballantine Belles Inc, presented "We Remember Idlewild" at the Latin Quarters in December 1987. The show was three days, December 11th and 12th at 8:30 p.m. and Sunday, December 13th at 4:30 p.m.

The Latin Quarters were a sell-out all three days with buses loaded with old-timers coming from places such as Chicago, Illinois, and Saginaw, Michigan.

The glamour, the style, the music, and the magic that was the Idlewild Revue was relived again in this show extravaganza.

The show featured Arthur Prysock with the Red Prysock Band. Also performing was vocalist Betty Joplin, The Sultans Tap Dancing act, the New Breed Be-Bop Society Orchestra conducted by Teddy Harris, Jr., also being featured in the band was bandleader Choker Campbell whose band often played Idlewild and traveled on the road with the show.

There was also the "Three Sixes Dancers," a group of very talented lady dancers who were and are still dancing in their ages of 50s-60s and I believe one dancer was even 70 years old.

Also on the show was The Fiesta Dolls; Rikki Ford and Carlean Gill from the original Idlewild Revue; The Ballantine Belles Youth Chorus line and singer Kim Weston.

The show was written by Beatrice Buck and was directed and choreographed by the now-late Clifford Fears. The show was emceed by Ed McKenzie. Ali Detroiters should remember Ed McKenzie and the "dance parties."

The proceeds from the show were partially sponsored by a grant from the Michigan Council for The Arts. It was to benefit the Dinah Washington Memorial Scholarship Fund created by the late singer to aid the talented (underprivileged) students desiring a career in the performing arts.

The show was a success. So much of a success that it was repeated in its entirety at a later date at the Masonic Auditorium for another two shows.

In the 60s, I remember Larry Steele bringing the show to Detroit. It was a very large show of entertainment. The show took many talented dancers and entertainers when it left Detroit to travel all over the States.

Local talent included Aretha Franklin and Freda Payne. I remember those good old party days, bright lights, traveling around the world and living in different cities. Detroit is a city of so many great opportunities to succeed in life. That is, if you want to make something of yourself. I would hear people say, "If you can't make it in Detroit, you can't make it."

I was raised just outside of Detroit and danced in the bright lights all over the world. What happens when the lights go out, and the parties are over? What else can you do for a living? I found out that without enough education you won't go far, regardless of how well you can dance.

I went back to school and from a professional dancer and show girl, to become a writer-author-teacher in a cosmetology public school vocational education and co-owner and director of a cosmetology school. Then I became a State of Michigan Examiner for the Department of Rules and Regulations of Cosmetology in which I conducted exams for graduate students seeking their cosmetology license.

After all the glitter, bright lights. What now, show girl? What about the future? Stop the show business, get married, get divorced. I have a wonderful son, Tony, who went into the medical field.

I need a new job. What will it be? Tony and I lived in an apartment after my divorce, in Highland Park, Michigan.

Show girl seeking employment.

Well, I made an appointment with Mayor Blackwell, the Mayor of Highland Park. (Did I have nerve or what!)

As I walked into his office, the mayor asked, "What is it I can do for you, Miss Ford?"

The mayor just sat and stared at me for a while (both of us silent). When he did speak, his words were, "You made this appointment with me because you need a job?"

"Yes," I replied, "I'm in a desperate situation. I just rented an apartment in your city three days ago. I had just enough money for a deposit and the first month's rent. I have a small son and I need a job today."

Again, the mayor was silent.

"Miss Ford," he said, "I have never known anyone to go about getting a job this way, so I suppose you indeed need a job. One of my duties today is going to be to help you as much as I can to see that you get some help in finding that job."

The mayor picked up the phone and called into his office a man I am going to call Mr. Johnson. The mayor told Mr. Johnson, "I want you to take Miss Ford to your office and if you have any opening of jobs that you feel she is qualified, please see that she gets an interview."

That day after an interview at Highland Park Hospital, I became an admitting emergency room clerk.

About ten days later, my new co-workers were all in array. "The mayor is here. He's asking for Miss Ford." He smiled as we talked. "I just came by to check on you. How do you like your new job?"

When the hospital closed, a resident doctor went onto his own practice and asked me to become part of his office staff. I worked as a receptionist for this orthopedic for some years. It was great and I learned so much.

When I was ready for a change, my doctor asked me what I would like as a professional change. I told him I had always wanted to go into cosmetology. While in show business, I had become fairly good with make-up and hairstyling.

That next week, Doc and I were sitting in the office of one of Detroit's best-known beauty schools, where Doc paid my tuition in full (for being a good employee).

Graduated "Licensed Cosmetologist."

Graduated "Cosmetology Teacher."

Became a featured writer of cosmetology articles for a well-known beauty magazine.

Became part owner of a beauty school.

Now as I grow older, I am still practicing in my chosen career as Beauty School Senior Unlimited Instructor and theory teacher. I am enjoying each day as I see the young students, I have helped train graduate and become well-known professionals.

I thank you with all my heart, Doc.

I also thank my present employer and coworkers who make going to work a pleasure each day.

My present employment has taken me from the busy hustle and bustle of the big city. I have moved up to North Michigan.

I find myself not too far from my show business roots, Idlewild, Michigan, just about 1 $ hours away.

On my vacation, I went there for a visit. The same great feeling of beauty and peace overcame me. Still in my heart are memories of Idlewild. As I drive through town, I have this longing of wanting to stay.

Idlewild is still part of my roots. My aunt bought a home and retired in Idlewild after she visited me one summer. My son spent summer vacations in Idlewild.

While on a vacation visit to Idlewild, I rented a room at the Morton Motel. It is hard for me to explain the feeling that has become a part of me and Idlewild, but "it's just some kind of wonderful!"

I have gone as far as getting a listing of property for sale and a friend, John Meeks, has sponsored me as a member and I joined the Mid-Michigan Idlewild Association. I am enjoying all activities.

I was given a copy of the sheet music "Idlewild Song"

given to me by my friend John Meeks, who told me the song was written back in 1927. With the help of my sister Gwen, the song, music, and lyrics were put on tape. I played and presented the song to my club members (Mid-Michigan Idlewilders). I also presented and played the taped song Idlewild's community officials at the Idlewild Historic and Cultural Center on August 12th, 1999.

This was the first time anyone present had heard the song or knew the music existed.

Later that day, there were pictures taken and an article written in the local newspaper, "The Star."

Also present was Nellie Blue, who agreed to play the piano,

Copies of the sheet music were handed out and all present joined in and sang.

"Another wonderful experience in Idlewild."

The Last Chapter

Happy at last. I'm with the very first love of my life, "Ernest." I fell in love the very first time I saw him. I was about thirteen years old when he came into my life. He came to our house to see my brothers, I think. But when I first looked into his eyes, my heart seemed to skip a beat. He smiled at me with those beautiful gray eyes, and from that moment to the present (50 years later) I still feel that same attraction. Ernest lived with my sister Gwen and brother-in-law Henderson for a while. He worked with my brother Paul and my uncle Richard at Farm Crest Bakery in Detroit. Later he moved back to Chicago.

In between these fifty years, Ernest and I would see each other when he came for visits. We were friends. I knew I was too young for Ernest. This being my first love made me care for him more. Then came the day when Ernest called to say he was getting married and would be bringing his future wife to meet our family. I remember sitting at the dining room table in the corner feeling so sad inside I think I cried. His wife-to-be was so pretty, and everyone liked her so much. They were all happy for Ernest. I guess I was too, except I was wishing it was me. I remember telling my mom how I hoped I would marry a man like Ernest. She told me I was young, and I would have lots of time and had to grow and experience life more. But all through those life experiences, I never felt the feeling I have always felt for Ernest. Ernest and I have both married others (a few times), but both ended up alone.

I think prayer has brought us together. I say prayer has brought us together and I really believe this. At 63 years old living alone (by choice, of course), I refused to live with anyone anymore just because I was lonely. I was praying and I asked God to please help me. Let me have someone in my life I could be happy with and share the rest of my life.

Then one day Ernest called me. Ernest was alone also. Our first time together after so many years is so wonderful. One reason is because we liked each other from the beginning, then we were friends, then lovers. Now we enjoy each other so. I enjoy him and I am so happy. I love him so much. Ernest says he's going to marry me, and we will share this last chapter of our lives together. Our families know each other, and I am looking forward to sharing family time. In fact, our family members on both sides were planning a trip to Idlewild during Idlewild weekend. Now ain't that just some kind of wonderful?

The Early Years
Ernest & Rikki 1977

With Nat King Cole and friend, L:
John D. Chamberlain, 1963.

all
for
ex-
ny
%
er-
ed
)er
in
an.
fa-
is-
in
of

Idlewild in the '60s. There were many entertainers before me. But some I have worked on shows with are Four Tops, George Kirby, Jerry Butler, Brook Benton, Jackie Wilson, Bone Walker, Bill Doggett Band, Big Mable, and Della Reese for producer Arthur Braggs at the Paradise Club. He was from Saginaw, Michigan. I also became a member of the Idlewild club, founded by John Meeks. It was named (Mid-Michigan Idlewilders). In 1998, Idlewilders had a membership roster of forty members, I became number forty. Since then, membership has grown. Members from Detroit, Chicago, California, Saginaw, Lansing, Cleveland, and many other states.

THE BEIGE BEAUTS

Modern American Girls and Boys
On Stage, Deauville Hotel, Miami Beach

Smart Affairs girls on Larry's Prize-winning Float in
"Miss America" Beauty Pageant Parade, Atlantic City, N.J., 1962

BEN ALTEN'S
CLUB HARLEM
ATLANTIC CITY, NEW JERSEY

JACK SOUTHERN—MGR.

•

LARRY STEELE'S
"SMART AFFAIRS of '67"

STARRING
CAB CALLOWAY
JUNE 23—JULY 10

SAMMY DAVIS
JULY 11-17

DAMITA JO
JULY 18-27 AUGUST 21-24

BILLY DANIELS
JULY 28—AUGUST 10

LESLIE UGGAMS
AUGUST 11-20

THE TRENIERS
AUGUST 25—SEPTEMBER 3

LOU RAWLS
SEPTEMBER 4-10

AND EXTRA ADDED ATTRACTION FOR THE RUN OF THE PLAY
SLAPPY WHITE
AND FEATURING
**THE STRONG BROS. • MARIAN TAYLOR • THE TAPATEERS
COOK & BROWN • CHRIS CALLOWAY • SHIRLEY MAY
THE CONSTELLATIONS • DONALD FONTAINE**

AND HIGHLIGHTING THE MOST GORGEOUS AND TALENTED DANCING LADIES IN THE UNIVERSE
THE MODERN AMERICAN GIRLS

WITH THE MUSIC OF
JOHNNY LYNCH & HIS ORCHESTRA

Lon Fontaine, former "Smart Affairs" specialty feature act was choreographer for earlier editions.

C. FONTAINE
ured Dancer and one of the
art Affairs" Choreographers

Lyle Smith
Production Aide & Choreographer
Captain of Dancing & Show Girls

Walter Winchell and Larry at 1964 Democratic Convention in Atlantic City, N.J.

Walter Winchell with Larry and Korean singing star Lee Sohn ... Atlantic City, 1964.

With NAACP's Roy Wilkins, 1964

Larry with The Great Lady Of The Entertainment World, Lena Horne . . . 1956 at the Dunes Hotel, Las Vegas.

Nancy Wilson

JACKIE WILSON

Al Hibbler
Smart Affairs '57

Roy Hamilton appeared in several
editions of "Smart Affairs".

Jerry Butler was featured in "Smart Affairs '65".

Sir Lionel Beckels

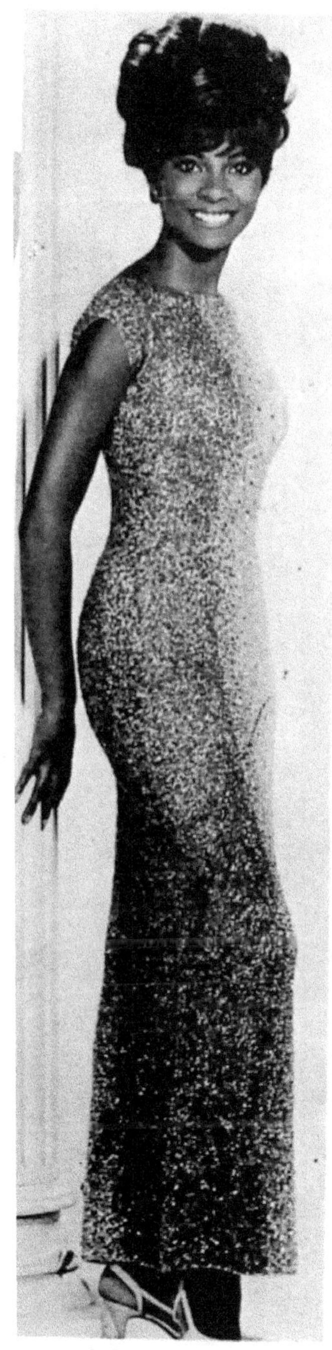

Leslie Uggams
"Smart Affairs '67"

The Divine One, Sarah Vaughan

LOLA FALANA

Paradise Club.

GEORGE PHIL GILES, SR.

PHIL GILES FLAMINGO BAR

Calvin (Eagle Eye) Shields

No. 340 – While in Idlewild, visit the beautiful CLUB EL MOROCCO——Food
served day and night (24 hours). Dine and Dance by wonderful music. Rooms
and Cottages available.

ARTHUR BRAGG'S 1962
IDLEWILD REVUE
THE INTERNATIONALLY FAMOUS REVUE

FEATURING

THE BEIGE BEAUTS

and

THE BEAUTIFUL HARLEM GIRLS

NO COVER
NO MINIMUM

IN THE HEART OF MONTREAL

Black Orchid
CASINO
892 ST. CATHERINE W.

The Vagabond Room Presents ★ ★ ★ ★
ARTHUR BRAGGS' 1963 Idlewild Revue
★ ★ WITH THE ★ ★
Rhythm Kings
Choker Campbell's
★ INTERNATIONAL TWIST BAND
AND 36 ALL STAR PERFORMERS AT TALENT'S TOPS
Beautiful Girls! Girls!
Glamorous Costumes,
Singers, Dancers, Thrills!
DANCE—SEASON'S BIGGEST, BEST EVENT
10 NITES—FRI., SEPT. 28, THRU SUN., OCT. 7
THE VAGABOND ROOM ★
"FINEST NIGHT CLUB IN OHIO"
10550 EUCLID AVE., CLEVELAND, OHIO
PHONE CE 1-3545 or 231-9534

ORCHID ROOM
12th and VINE
ARTHUR BRAGGS-
1960 IDLEWILD REVUE
STARRING
EARL GRANT
WITH
• FIESTA DOLLS • THE BRAGGETTES
MONA DESMOND • THE 4 TOPS
THE 3 RHYTHM KINGS
Plus
COUNT BELCHER AND HIS DETROIT ALL STARS
Phone HA. 1-8898 For Reservations
STARTING DECEMBER 21
THROUGH NEW YEARS EVE

Ornament: Resembling curvy, modern version of the shiny ornaments which graced hoods of older model autos, model Rikki Fort strikes up relaxed pose atop streamlined, 1961 Dodge Dart Phoenix convertible in Detroit, where she paid a recent visit to Dodge Division of the Chrysler Corp.

MOVING UP
Winsome, wil-
lowy and imbued
with show busi-
ness ambitions,
Detroiter Mar-
gueritha Ford,
18, is making her
debut this sea-
son as a show-
girl in Arthur
Bragg's Idlewild
Revue. A part-
time model, Mar-
gueritha, stands
5.10½; her aes-
thetic assets read
36-26-38.
Isaac Sutton

MOVING FAST — Gabriel Schonberg, left, proprietor of Savepte Drug Store, tells Rikkie Ford and Baker Johnson, company representatives, how fast the new popular priced Benson and Hedges cigarettes are moving in Detroit.

(First)
One of my jobs in Detroit---Representative forBenson and Hedges

Cigarettes

"IDLEWILD"
Song, One-Step and Tango Dance.
By
MAJ. N. CLARK SMITH
(Bac. A.M. Mus.)
CHICAGO
DEFENDER
BANDMASTER.
LYON & HEALY INC. — CHICAGO
5
Full Band and Orchestra Arrangements 50¢ each

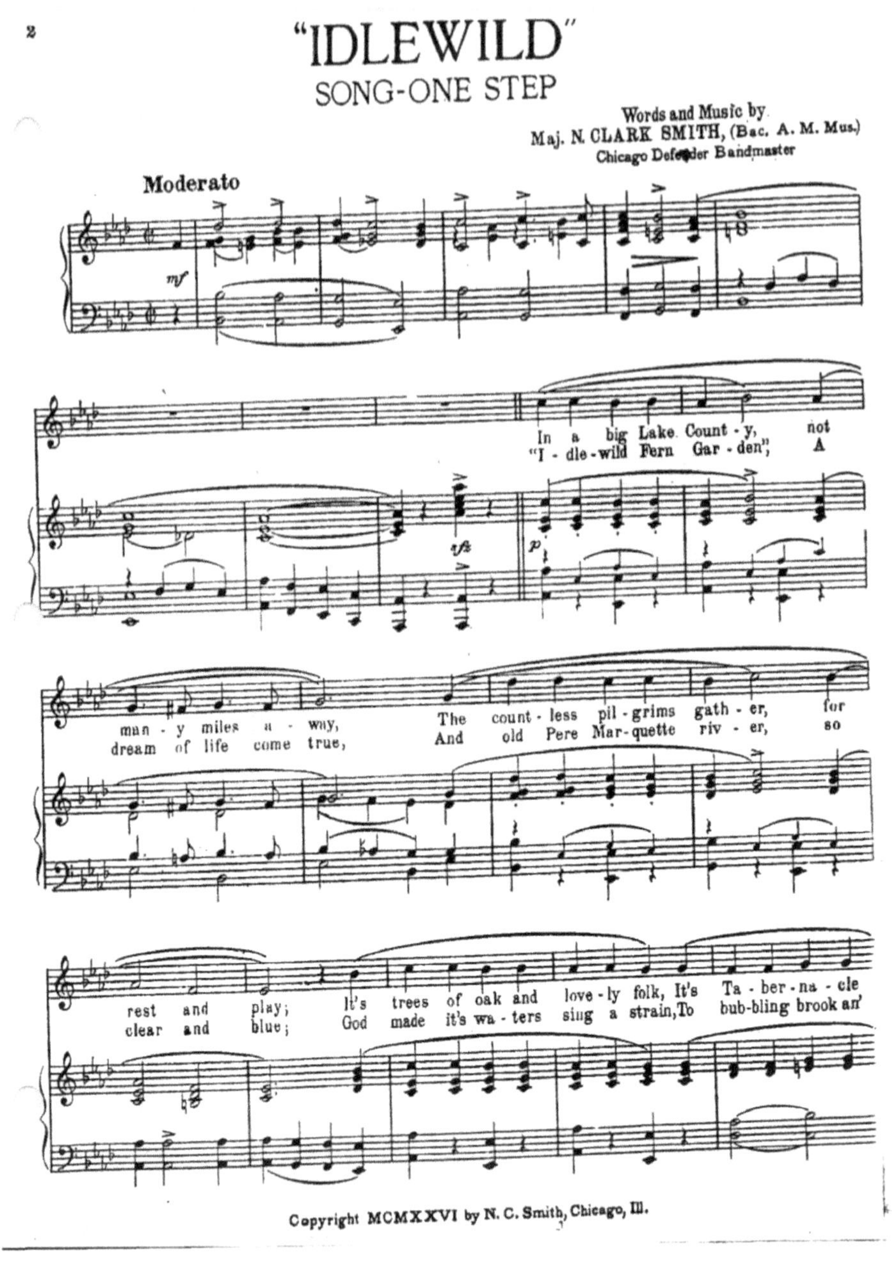
2
"IDLEWILD"
SONG-ONE STEP
Words and Music by
Maj. N. CLARK SMITH, (Bac. A. M. Mus.)
Chicago Defender Bandmaster
Moderato
mf
sfz
p
In a big Lake Count - y, not man - y miles a - way, The count - less pil - grims gath - er, for rest and play; It's trees of oak and love - ly folk, It's Ta - ber - na - cle
"I - dle - wild Fern Gar - den", A dream of life come true, And old Pere Mar-quette riv - er, so clear and blue; God made it's wa - ters sing a strain, To bub-bling brook an'
Copyright MCMXXVI by N. C. Smith, Chicago, Ill.

or a church, Where ma-ples grow with state-ly birch, 'Tis na-ture's won-der-child. Dear
spring re-main, They chant and sing a sweet re-frain, With na-tures mu-sic dream.
CHORUS
I dle-wild my I-dle-wild, I hear the birds a-
call-ing, I feel the dew-drops fall-ing; To I - dle-wild, Dear
I - dle-wild, The can-dle lights a-burn-ing, My thoughts of love are turn-ing, To
1
2
I - dle - wild. (Oh boy,) Dear wild.
p-f
sf
IDLEWILD 3

Duett Chorus: Tango Dance

IDLEWILD RESORT CO.   WILBUR M. LEMON, Manager
Suite 866 Hartford Building   CHICAGO, ILL.   O. S. Dearborn Street
RAYNER, DALHEIM & CO.
MUSIC PRINTERS
CHICAGO

Ballantine Belle's INC.
"We Remember Idlewild" Part II
SPECIAL
BLACK HISTORY CELEBRATION

FEATURING
CAST OF 50

SINGING
* THE NEW FIESTA DOLLS
* ORIGINAL 3-6's dancers
* TEDDY HARRIS & his NEW BREED BE-BOP SOCIETY ORCHESTRA
TAP DANCING
SOLOISTS

CHORUS GIRLS
THE FOUR SULTANS
* VOCALIST BETTY JOPLIN
ARTHUR PRYSOCK
CARLEAN GILL
RIKKI FORD
THREE GENERATIONS of DANCING
THE TAP DANCING SULTANS

The GLAMOUR, MUSIC AND MAGIC THAT WAS
THE IDLEWILD REVUE WILL LIVE AGAIN AT THE
MASONIC TEMPLE

Written and Produced by
BEATRICE BUCK

Directed and Choreographed
CLIFFORD FEARS

MASONIC TEMPLE'S
SCOTTISH RITE CATHEDRAL
* KIM WESTON
500 TEMPLE
SATURDAY FEBRUARY 27, 1988
8:00 P.M.
SUNDAY FEBRUARY 28, 1988
4:00P.M.

TICKETS
$10.00
$15.00

Michigan Council
for the Arts

WE REMEMBER IDLEWILD

"HELLO TO IDLEWILD" . . . . Entire Cast

"HONKY TONK" . . . . Teddy Harris, Jr. Orchestra
CHOKER CAMPBELL, Guest Conductor

THE TAP DANCE. . . . . The Sultans

SPECIAL SELECTIONS . . . . Kim Weston

"SOFT" . . . . The Three Sixes Dancers, The New Fiesta Dolls,
Belle's Youth Chorus

FEATURING RED PRYSOCK ON TENOR SAXAPHONE

– 10 MINUTE INTERMISSION –

"WE'VE GOT A LOT OF LIVING TO DO". . . . . The Three Sixes Dancers

THE SOUND OF THE SAXAPHONE . . . . Red Prysock and Band

VOCAL RENDITIONS. . . . . Betty Joplin

MEET OUR STAR. . . . . ARTHUR PRYSOCK

FINALE . . . . Entire Cast

KIM WESTON, M.C.

All Musical Arrangements by TEDDY HARRIS, JR. The Ballantine Belles, Inc. Musical Conductor

All production numbers created and choreographed by CLIFFORD FEARS

The Executive Producer is the BALLANTINE BELLES, INC.   KIM WESTON, ARTISTIC DIRECTOR

"HELLO TO IDLEWILD", Composed by Beatrice Buck who wrote the Production and Produced the Entire Program.

All dance costumes were designed by Floretta Johnson. The Three Sixes dance costumes were designed by Beatrice Buck and made by Denise R. (Cookie) Crapps.

The costumes for "SOFT" were done especially for this production from a design of a costume loaned to the Ballantine Belles by LON FONTAINE of New York. Mr. Fontaine is a former member of the original Idlewild Revue.

This souvenir booklet was designed and compiled by MAMIE SHEPARD.

Directed by CLIFFORD FEARS.

The Ballantine Belle's Inc.
present

WE REMEMBER IDLEWILD
Latin Quarters
December 11 - 12 - 13, 1987

During all of the shows, the job of the show girls was to look beautiful, while the dancers and other acts were simply talented. The chorus girls danced in high heel shoes. When it was time to "Bury the show" in Idlewild, the day after Labor Day, one of the final treats for their audience, in addition to some great movement and vocal performances, was when the singers would become the dancers and the dancers would become the singers. Arthur Braggs' Idlewild Revue toured the United States and Canada where they performed in Detroit at the Flame Show Bar and Zombies in Paradise Valley, in Chicago at Robert's Show Lounge, the Tivoli Theater, and Club Delisa; at the Apollo Theater and Wilt Chamberlain's Small Paradise Café in Harlem; at The Orchid Room in Kansas City, Missouri; The Pink Poodle in Indianapolis; the Vagabond Room in Cleveland, Ohio, and other venues in Boston, Washington D.C., Baltimore, Philadelphia, Buffalo, Kansas City, Kansas, and Oklahoma; as well as the Black Orchid in the Canadian metropolitan areas of Montreal, Toronto, and Quebec City. They performed at many of the popular nightspots in those cities. Brags along with Ziggy Johnson directed Arthur Braggs Idlewild Revue, while Tommy Roy, a popular radio personality for WKLA in Ludington, handled publicity, promotion, and public relations.

I am not trying to give the history of Idlewild only my experience of some of the entertainment and reminiscences of my time spent there.

I once read that in the 1900s there were about 85% White, about 13 % African Americans, maybe 94% Native Americans, and maybe 1% Asian Americans.

Because of segregation, Black Americans were not allowed at White resorts.

Idlewild became known as a "Black Resort." I remember my mother going to Idlewild to fish and hunt. See her dressed in a hunting suit, with a rifle, remembering she was Choctaw Indian. The oldest of ten children. Her father also inspired her. Her father rode in the rodeo and my mother rode the barrels, in Mississippi. Her sister bought a home in Idlewild after seeing me in a show in Idlewild at the Paradise Club. I became a part of Idlewild in the '60s. There were many entertainers before me. But some I have worked on shows with are Four Tops, George Kirby, Jerry Butler, Brook Benton, Jackie Wilson, Bone Walker, Bill Doggett Band, Big Mable, and Della Reese for producer Arthur Braggs at the Paradise Club. He was from Saginaw, Michigan. I also became a member of the Idlewild Club, founded by John Meeks. It was named (Mid-Michigan Idlewilders). In 1998, Idlewilders had a membership roster of forty members, I became number forty. Since then membership has grown. Members from Detroit, Chicago, California, Saginaw, Lansing, Cleveland, and many other states.